TOM BUCHAN

CRITICAL RACE THEORY AND LBGTQ+ IN PUBLIC EDUCATION: A Path to Disaster
A Very Short Introduction

First edition

This book was professionally typeset on Reedsy.
Find out more at reedsy.com

Contents

1

Chapter One: Introduction

I am writing this very short introduction to Critical Race Theory (CRT) {Now being rebranded as Culturally Responsive Teaching} and LGBTQ+ in schools to provide the reader with a clearer understanding of what it is and is not.

I have been a public-school teacher for sixteen years and an online/remote teacher for public & private schools for three years. I have seen the abuse of CRT and other types of indoctrination in the classroom, and it has nothing to do with critical thinking, which should the at the core of any elementary, middle, and high school curriculum.

Public education has been under assault for decades by the progressive left, and there are no signs that this will stop. Remember students in schools singing hymns to President Obama when he was first elected president?[1] In fact, it keeps getting worse, and CRT is the latest progressive attack on critical thinking in public education. There has been a backlash against CRT, with many states banning it outright.[2] This might be one of the reasons for the possible rebranding to Culturally Responsive Teaching. It is also one of the many reasons that parents are pulling their kids out of public schools and putting them in private schools or homeschooling them.

Meanwhile, school administrators and teachers are denying that CRT is being taught.[3] They are partially correct. More on that later.

This little book is in no way meant to be taken as an exhaustive study, but hopefully, it will provide the reader with some information on who supports CRT, who is against it, and why. As well as some of the facts and lies from both sides in order for the reader to become more aware of CRT, do further research, and become more informed.

My opinion regarding the subject is obvious from the subtitle: 'A Path to Disaster.'

2

Chapter Two: What Is Critical Race Theory?

Critical race theory came about in the mid-1970s, when a hand full of lawyers, activists, and legal scholars in the U.S, began thinking that many of the important advances of the civil rights movement of the 1960s had slowed down and, in some cases, were beginning to dissolve. This led some early writers on the subject, such as Derrick Bell, Alan Freeman, and Richard Delgado, to attempt to remedy the situation and reinvigorate the cause. They believed that more devious and widespread forms of racism were deeply embedded in the American system. This form of CRT is an academic movement of civil rights scholars who critically examine laws and legislation and how they intersect with race issues. Many in the field became determined to root out what they consider to be this systemic racism. This is where the problems began. Much of the controversy surrounding CRT today goes beyond its validity as an academic movement and has become a questionable activist movement. From this perspective, CRT is being used in schools of education, political science, sociology, and philosophy. When it comes to education, with which this book is concerned, it is used to understand & radically revamp school discipline

3

and hierarchy issues, affirmative action, high-stakes testing, written and verbal expression, controversies regarding curriculum and history, and bilingual and multicultural education, and other areas as they pop up.

Proponents of CRT believe it is an essential part of a historically aware education, while

opponents claim that its premises are factually wrong and will significantly damage education, students, and our nation as a whole.

Critical Race Theory: An Introduction, by Richard Delgado and Jean Stefancic, is considered by many to be a seminal book in CRT. It was first published in 2001 and is currently in its third edition. Unfortunately, the book contains no footnotes or references. I find this bizarre because both of the authors are law school professors and should recognize the importance of references in any scholarly work. All they offer for support, if one can call it that, are lists of "Suggested Readings" at the end of the chapters. Moreover, Delgado and Stefancic make many concrete and controversial claims with no citations. For example: "Police shooting and killings of unarmed black men have risen so rapidly that even a leading medical journal recognizes them as growing health concerns" (p. 124). This requires supporting evidence. How many shootings were recorded ten years ago? How many shootings were recorded recently? Which medical journal made the statement, when they made it, and how do they define a 'health concern'? The authors also make claims about the frequency of racial profiling, the unreliability of standardized test scores, and the validity of the implicit association test,[4] to name a few, and expect the reader to take them at their word. In short, this is propaganda. When it comes to theory, the book is fairly adequate, but when it comes to empirical evidence, the authors provide none, and this is a major concern regarding the book's validity.

CONCEPTS AND INSIGHTS SERIES®
Critical Race
Theory
A Primer
Khiara M. Bridges
FOUNDATION
PRESS

Khiara Bridges provides some of the key tenets of CRT in her book Critical Race Theory: A Primer:

- Racism is a normal feature of society and is embedded within systems and institutions that replicate racial inequality. Racist incidents are manifestations of structural and systemic racism.
- Racism is codified in law, embedded in structures, and woven into public policy. CRT rejects claims of meritocracy or "colorblindness" and recognizes that it is the systemic nature of racism that bears primary responsibility for reproducing racial inequality.
- CRT seeks to embrace the lived experiences of people of color, including those preserved through storytelling, and the history of black intellectuals who have contributed to the anti-racist movement.
- Race is not biologically real but is socially constructed and socially significant. It recognizes that science (as demonstrated in the Human Genome Project) refutes the idea of biological racial differences. Race is the product of social thought and is not connected to biological reality.
- CRT rejects the focus on 'fixing" individuals and instead fixing oppressive and disabling systems.

Meanwhile, the University of Tennessee, a member of the Critical Race Collective (CRC), makes an attempt to be a little succinct with its five key tenets:[5]

1. ***Centrality of Race and Racism in Society:*** CRT asserts that racism is a central component of American life.
2. ***Challenge to Dominant Ideology:*** CRT challenges the claims of neutrality, objectivity, colorblindness, and meritocracy in society.
3. ***Centrality of Experiential Knowledge:*** CRT asserts that the experi-

ential knowledge of people of color is appropriate, legitimate, and an integral part to analyzing and understanding racial inequality.

4. ***Interdisciplinary Perspective:*** CRT challenges ahistoricism and the unidisciplinary focuses of most analyses and insists that race and racism be placed in both a contemporary and historical context using interdisciplinary methods.

5. ***Commitment to Social Justice:*** CRT is a framework that is committed to a social justice agenda to eliminate all forms of subordination of people.

Both of these sets of tenets are so loaded with jargon that they can be used in many ways, most of which I propose are disastrous for public education. Since UT is less verbose, I will tackle these tenets and also point out some differences.

The first in both sets is the clearest; racism is systemic, i.e., it affects everything in American life.

The second tenets challenge not just those "claims" but also the idea that they are worthwhile aspirations. "Meritocracy" is considered to be entirely false and inherently racist and wants to eliminate it as a goal or standard. CRT wants to substitute color awareness and eliminate "colorblindness. The same goes for objectivity and neutrality, which are defined as white values and therefore inherently racist. This tenet is also strange because it seems to run against Martin Luther King Jr's "Dream" when he famously said, "I have a dream that my four little children will one day live in a nation where they will not be judged by the color of their skin but by the content of their character" So, does this mean that Dr. King Jr. was a racist.

The third tenet in both I don't think anyone would disagree with on the surface; however, what CRT claims is that "experiential knowledge" is much more significant than the collection, analysis, interpretation, and presentation of quantitative data; i.e., anecdotal evidence (which, among can be misconstrued or even completely wrong even if a sincere one) is far more important than anything else, and only the anecdotal evidence of "people of color" has validity.

The fourth tenet is so incoherent that I can't figure out what they are claiming, except to change history by bringing in a perspective that makes history into whatever they want it to depict, e.g., the New York Times and Nicole Hannah Jones' 1619 Project, which has been widely debunked by major historians. (Its most absurd claim is that the American Revolution was fought to protect slavery.)[6]

The fifth tenet is equally bizarre. What is "social justice?" According to Human Rights Careers, it has four essential goals (tenets): "*Social justice* is fairness as it manifests in society. That includes human rights, access [to resources], participation, and equity."[7] The Corporate Finance Institute throws out a fifth tenet for good measure. Diversity: to expand opportunities for marginalized or disadvantaged groups[8], i.e., affirmative action. I have no idea what "social justice" is, but I love Thomas Sowell's quotes about it.[9]

3

Chapter Three: CRT in the Classroom

Many argue that CRT is not taught in public schools.[10] Technically, this is true, and there is no evidence that the theory is being taught to students; however, teachers are being taught to use CRT in their classrooms[11] (the activist part of the movement mentioned above). This is obvious from the plethora of workshops, professional development sessions, ready-made lesson plans for students, and instructional materials for teachers. For example, Last summer (2021), the Manhattan Institute's Christopher Rufo reported that 30 public school districts in 15 states are teaching a book, *Not My Idea*.[12]

Here are some excerpts: "White supremacy has been lying to kids for centuries" (57). "Whiteness is a bad deal. It always was" (58).

The book also provides a contract: "Binding You to WHITENESS You Get:

Stolen land, stolen riches, special favors* WHITENESS Gets: to mess endlessly with the lives of your friends, neighbors, loved ones, and all fellow humans of COLOR for the purpose of profit. *Land, riches, and favors may be revoked at any time, for any reason" (59). In short, Whiteness and white supremacy run rampant, and all people of color are helpless victims of this scourge that plagues our nation.

Plenty of other examples prove racial essentialism and collective guilt are being taught to young students. In Cupertino, California, an elementary school required third graders to rank themselves according to the "power and privilege" associated with their ethnicities.[13] Schools in Buffalo, New York, taught students that "all white people" perpetuate "systemic racism" and had kindergarteners watch a video of dead black children, warning them about "racist police and state-sanctioned violence." And in Arizona, the state's education department sent out an "equity toolkit" to schools that claimed infants as young as 3 months old can start to show signs of racism and "remain strongly biased in favor of whiteness" by age 5."[14] This is some pretty outrageous stuff that is being used to indoctrinate elementary and middle school students.

And then there is Culturally Responsive Teaching, which, according to ShaQuina Stanley, the owner and founder of Hip Hop Teaching, "…is a method of instruction that seeks to incorporate the unique and diverse cultural backgrounds of each individual student. Instead of seeking to explain the world around us, CRT in this context allows us to appreciate and include the diversity that exists within the United States of America. Some of the many cultural outlets created by black and brown communities throughout history include ***hip hop, AAVE, code-switching, food, and ethnic offshoots of pop culture.*** These elements should be used by numerous teachers across the country to best connect with students of varying cultural backgrounds."[15]

I think everyone knows what hip hop and food are, but what about the other "cultural outlets"? AAVE stands for African American Vernacular English, which is an informal dialect spoken by many African Americans in the United States. For examples, see the table below.[16]

By the way, if you are white and use AAVE, be aware that you might be a racist; go figure. "When white people use terms that are part of AAVE, it erases the history behind it."[17] What does that even mean?

Code-switching (CS) is the practice of moving back and forth between two languages or between two dialects or registers of the same language at one time.[18] For example switching from Standard American Language to African American Vernacular English or vice versa. This occurs more frequently in conversation than in writing. As for "ethnic offshoots of pop culture," your guess is as good as mine, and I have no clue.

"As its name should make abundantly clear, Critical Race Theory (CRT) is the child of Critical Theory (CT), or, to be more precise, its grandchild. Critical Theory is the immediate forebearer of Critical *Legal* Theory (CLT), and CLT begat CRT."[19]

In the end, Critical Race Theory, Culturally Responsive Teaching, Affirmative Action, Diversity Training, Sensitivity Training, Safe Places, Cultural Appropriation, and on and on are nothing more than attempts by the Marxist, progressive left to support victimhood for people of color, drive wedges between people and cultures creating a balkanization of America, spreading socialism, collectivism, and the white supremacy narrative, identity politics, relativism, and intolerance of anyone who dares to disagree with them. Also, by telling people that they are not individuals but are a monolith driven by forces that they do not understand, as in the case of Robin Diangelo in her racist diatribe *White Fragility: Why It's So Hard for White People to Talk About Racism:*

"When a racial group's collective prejudice is backed by the power of legal authority and institutional control, it is transformed into racism, a far-reaching system that functions independently from the intentions or self-images of individual actors." Pg. 20

When all the while denying liberty, freedom of speech, individual responsibility, property rights, and developing a moral and honest character. I prefer Shelby Steele's outlook on racism from *White Guilt: How Blacks and Whites Together Destroyed the Promise of the Civil Rights Era.*

WHITE GUILT

HOW BLACKS AND WHITES TOGETHER DESTROYED THE PROMISE OF THE CIVIL RIGHTS ERA

SHELBY STEELE

AUTHOR OF THE *NEW YORK TIMES* BESTSELLER
THE CONTENT OF OUR CHARACTER

"Possibly white guilt's worst effect is that it does not permit whites- and nonwhites to appreciate something extraordinary: the fact that ·whites in America, and even elsewhere in the West, have achieved a truly remarkable moral transformation. One is forbidden to speak thus, but it is simply true. There are no serious advocates of white supremacy in America today because see this idea as morally repugnant. If there is still the odd white bigot out there surviving past his time, there are millions of whites who only feel goodwill toward minorities" (Pg.12).

Black conservatives are a small and silenced minority. Voices like Ben Carson, Brandon Tatum, Candace Owens, Larry Elder, Joel Patrick, the Hodge twins, and Shelby Steele himself are called Uncle Toms and race traitors for choosing to think outside the box that our society had placed Black people into. In the words of Joe Biden: "You ain't black if you don't vote Democrat."

Progressive liberalism tells Black conservatives they are not allowed to consider the statistics, offer realistic solutions for their community, or stand up for family values; or else they will be named as traitors to their community - how can we stand for this obvious oppression? And let's ask ourselves - why does progressive liberalism silence Black conservatives? Control? Power? You be the judge.

Race exists only to serve racism, and as such, racism continues. But if we can stand apart from the 500-year lie told to us, we might actually be able to see through the fog of racial ignorance and possibly, get a glimpse of a future we can scarcely imagine. It's possible, but we do need to have some difficult questions answered. Does this mean we ignore what race has done to people of color? No. Does this mean we are all now pure and cheerfully clean, capable of escaping the centuries of harm and destruction race has done and continues to do? No. Does it mean that if we finally step outside of race, to view race as an aberration of flawed human ideas so we can move forward in unity, compassion, charity, grace, and accountability? It's time to start thinking of our fellow humans not as blacks, whites, or any other race - but as brothers and sisters. One race, unified by our mutual humanity. We are only divided by what we let ourselves be divided by.

Chapter Three: What Is LGBTQ+

According to *Very Well Mind.com*, this is what the letters stand for:

- **L (Lesbian):** A lesbian is a woman/woman-aligned person who is attracted to only people of the same/similar gender.
- **G (Gay):** Gay is usually a term used to refer to men/men-aligned individuals who are only attracted to people of the same/similar gender. However, lesbians can also be referred to as gay. The use of the term gay became more popular during the 1970s. Today, bisexual and pansexual people sometimes use gay to casually refer to themselves when they talk about their similar gender attraction.
- **B (Bisexual):** Bisexual indicates an attraction to all genders. The recognition of bisexual individuals is important, since there have been periods when people who identify as bi have been misunderstood as being gay. Bisexuality has included transgender, binary and nonbinary individuals since the release of the "Bisexual Manifesto" in 1990.

- **T (Transgender):** Transgender is a term that indicates that a person's gender identity is different from the gender associated with the sex they were assigned at birth.
- **Q (Queer or Questioning):** Though queer may be used by people as a specific identity, it is often considered an umbrella term for anyone who is non-cisgender or heterosexual. But it is also a slur. It should not be placed on all members of the community, and should only be used by cisgender and heterosexual individuals when referring to a person who explicitly identifies with it. Questioning refers to people who may be unsure of their sexual orientation and/or gender identity.
- **+ (Plus):** The 'plus' is used to signify all of the gender identities and sexual orientations that are not specifically covered by the other five initials. An example is Two-Spirit, a pan-Indigenous American identity.[20]

I will leave the reader to research and come to their own decisions on the above.

5

Chapter Four: LGBTQ+ in the Classroom

Sex education in public schools today is inundated with LGBTQ+ sexuality, and the LGBTQ+ movement demands that homosexual relationships, and transgender, be presented to children as good, healthy, and equal in every way to hetero-sexuality.

This chapter will be entirely informational. I will supply articles for the reader to peruse, and you can come to your own conclusions.

• Some public schools teach children they could be born in the wrong body.[21]

• Young teens are shown videos with techniques to pleasure their sex partners.[22]

• Students are told how to get secret abortions without telling their parents.[23]

Homosexuality

In Austin, Texas, schools introduce sexual orientation and gender identity concepts to third graders and have sixth and seventh graders play a sexuality matching game with terms like "bisexual," "gay," "lesbian," and "homophobia."[24]

California law instructs public school teachers to emphasize homosexual relationships: "Teachers should… actively use examples of same-sex couples in class discussions."[25]

California officials insist that sex ed lessons be inclusive of sexual relationships with multiple partners.[26]

Transgender

Many public schools are beginning to teach the radical, anti-science proposition that biological sex is meaningless, that some kids are born in the wrong body, and that some girls have penises, and that boys can menstruate and get pregnant. The American College of Pediatricians calls this psychological child abuse.[27]

Fairfax County, Virginia, recently scrubbed its sex education materials of the concept that human beings have biologically-determined sex of male or female and replaced it with "sex assigned at birth."[28]

In Fairfax, sex ed lessons present transgenderism as a healthy sexual identity without mentioning the health and medical risks associated with so-called sex transition.[29]

In fact, curriculum drafters voted 12 times to exclude health risk information from student lessons.[30]

The new curriculum in Austin teaches middle school children that doctors assign sex to babies based on their genitalia but that "sex does NOT always match with their gender identity." Do not "assume that people with a penis are boys" because "someone with a penis might identify as a girl."[31]

Teachers in North Carolina are given comprehensive training on how to introduce transgender concepts into the minds of very young children, courtesy of the "Welcoming Schools" curriculum[32] created by the Human Rights Campaign, the nation's largest LGBTQ lobby.

Some school districts are beginning to teach LGBTQ+ history. The Southern Poverty Law Center (SPLC). has created a campaign for public schools called "Teaching Tolerance." "Teaching Tolerance" instructs history teachers on how to put a "queer" spin on nearly every major event in American history.[33]

All public schools in California[34], New Jersey[35], and Illinois[36] are now required to teach children LGBTQ+ history. In Illinois, schools are not even allowed to purchase history textbooks that fail to include an LGBTQ+ angle.

6

Chapter Five: Conclusion

So, there you have it. There is so much more information out there, so do your research and make up your mind. Is this the crap we want our public schools to indoctrinate our children with?

If you found this book helpful, I would greatly appreciate it if you left a favorable review for the book on Amazon.com. Thanks, T.M. Buchan

LATE BREAKING NEWS

California Public Ed Teacher Training Includes Pansexuality and a Semen Exercise

Alex Parker August 5, 2022

New Leader of Deep-Pocketed Critical Race Theory Group Wants to Defund the Police

Andrew Kerr, August 3, 2022

Notes

CHAPTER ONE: INTRODUCTION

1   "Obama Children Sing for Change for Dear Leader" October 1, 2008, accessed July 27, 2022, https://www.youtube.com/watch?v=54tjbgJmLFg

"Elementary School Students Taught Pro-Obama Songs" By Brian Montopoli September 24, 2009, accessed July 27, 2022, https://www.cbsnews.com/news/elementary-school-students-taught-pro-obama-songs/

"School Kids Brainwashed to Worship Obama." https://www.youtube.com/watch?v=K5UPFj8NCPY

2   "States That Have Banned Critical Race Theory 2022" https://worldpopulationreview.com/state-rankings/states-that-have-banned-critical-race-theory

3   Teaching Critical Race Theory Isn't Happening in Classrooms, Teachers Say in Survey." By Phil McCausland, July 1, 2021, accessed July 27, 2022, https://www.nbcnews.com/news/us-news/teaching-critical-race-theory-isn-t-happening-classrooms-teachers-say-n1272945

"Head of Teachers Union Says Critical Race Theory Isn't Taught in Schools, Vows to Defend 'Honest History'" https://www.cbsnews.com/news/critical-race-theory-teachers-union-honest-history/

CHAPTER TWO: WHAT IS CRITICAL RACE THEORY?

4   "IAT: Fad or fabulous?" Beth Azer, July/August 2008, Vol 39, No 7, accessed July 28, 2022, https://www.apa.org/monitor/2008/07-08/psychometric

"For Years, This Popular Test Measured Anyone's Racial Bias. But it Might Not Work After All. 'By Germain Lopez Mar 7, 2017, access July 28, 2022 https://www.vox.com/identities/2017/3/7/14637626/implicit-association-test-racism

5   "Critical Race Collective" The University of Tennessee, https://cssj.utk.edu/divisions/critical-race-collective/

6   "Twelve Scholars Critique the 1619 Project and the New York Times Magazine Editor Responds." January 26, 2020, accessed July 25, 2022, https://historynewsnet work.org/article/174140

7   "What Does Social Justice Mean?" By Human Rights Careers, accessed July 26,2022, https://www.humanrightscareers.com/issues/what-does-social-justice-mean/

8   "What is Social Justice?" By CFI Team, Updated May 8, 2022, accessed July 26, 2022, https://corporatefinanceinstitute.com/resources/knowledge/other/social-justice/

9   "Thomas Sowell Quotes About Social Justice." https://www.azquotes.com/author/13901-Thomas_Sowell/tag/social-justice

CHAPTER THREE: CRT IN THE CLASSROOM

10   "Teaching Critical Race Theory Isn't Happening in Classrooms, Teachers Say in Survey." By Phil McCausland, July 1, 2021, accessed July 26, 2022 https://www.n bcnews.com/news/us-news/teaching-critical-race-theory-isn-t-happening-class rooms-teachers-say-n1272945

National Teacher's Union President Is Accused of Gaslighting Parents by Saying Critical Race Theory Is NOT Taught in Schools and Prepares to Sue States Banning the Controversial Lessons." By Melissa Koenig, July 7, 2021, accessed July 26,2022, https://www.dailymail.co.uk/news/article-9763059/Teachers-union-president-says-CRT-NOT-taught-prepares-sue-states-banning-it.html

Teachers'-Union Head Claims CRT Is Only Taught at Colleges By BRITTANY BERNSTEIN, July 6, 2021, accessed July 26, 2022, https://www.nationalreview.co m/news/teachers-union-head-claims-crt-is-only-taught-at-colleges/

11   Education Consultant Uses Critical Race Theory to Train School Teachers, Staff According to Documents." By Kelsey Koberg, June 13, 2022, accessed July 26, 2022, https://www.msn.com/en-us/news/us/education-consultant-uses-critical-race-theory-to-train-school-teachers-staff-according-to-documents/ar-AAYq1aE

"Critical Race Theory in Public Schools." https://eric.ed.gov/?q=Critical+Race+Th eory+in+public+schools

"Results for CRT." Accessed July 26, 2022, https://www.teacherspayteachers.com/Browse/Search:crt

12   "Yes, Critical Race Theory Is Being Taught in Public Schools" Editorial by Washing-ton Examiner, July 12, 2021, accessed July 27, 2022, https://www.washingtonexam

iner.com/opinion/yes-critical-race-theory-is-being-taught-in-public-schools

CRT Chart https://twitter.com/realchrisrufo/status/1413292881264005126?s=2 0&t=Um6ndZEN0UR3S9XihpMDTA

13 "Woke Elementary." By Christopher F. Rufo, January 13, 2021, accessed July29, 2022, https://www.city-journal.org/identity-politics-in-cupertino-california-elementa ry-school

14 "Failure Factory." By Christopher F. Rufo, February 23, 2021, accessed July, 30, 2022, https://www.city-journal.org/buffalo-public-schools-critical-race-theory-curr iculum

15 'Critical Race Theory Vs. Culturally Responsive Teaching.' By ShaQuina Stanley, accessed July 30, 2022, https://www.hiphopteaching.com/culturally-responsive-teaching/

16 17 "What is AAVE?" By Alison Maciejewski Cortez, Updated May 10, 2022, accessed July30, 2022, https://blog.lingoda.com/en/what-is-aave/

What Is African American Vernacular English (AAVE)? By Richard Nordquist, Updated June 09, 2019, accessed July 2022, https://www.thoughtco.com/african-american-vernacular-english-aave-1689045

17 "What Is AAVE & Why White People Shouldn't Use It Flippantly." September 1, 2020, accessed July, 29, 2022, https://www.yourtango.com/2020336351/what-aave-why-white-people-shouldnt-use-flippantly

18 "Learn the Function of Code Switching as a Linguistic Term." By Richard Nordquist, Updated on July 25, 2019, accessed July 29, 2022, https://www.thoughtco.com/code-switching-language-1689858

19 "Critical Race Theory, the New Intolerance, and Its Grip on America." *Jonathan Butcher and Mike Gonzalez,* December 7, 2020, accessed July 29, 2022 https://ww w.heritage.org/civil-rights/report/critical-race-theory-the-new-intolerance-and-its-grip-america

CHAPTER THREE: WHAT IS LGBTQ+

20 "What Does LGBTQ+ Mean?" By Kendra Cherry, updated on July 18, 2022, accessed, July 29, 2022 https://www.verywellmind.com/what-does-lgbtq-mean-5069804

CHAPTER FOUR: LGBTQ+ IN THE CLASSROOM

21 John Domen, "Fairfax Co. school district passes proposals to modify sex ed, dress

codes," WTOP News, June 15, 2018, accessed August 1 , 2022, https://wtop.com/fai
rfax-county/2018/06/school-district-considers-changes-to-sex-ed-dress-codes/.

22 Clare Chretien, "Parents furious over obscene sex ed lesson for 14-year-olds:
The high school freshmen were taught about sex toys, and oral and anal sex,"
LifeSiteNews, May 1, 2018, accessed July 30, 2022, https://www.lifesitenews.c
om/news/parents-furious-after-sex-ed-lesson-for-14-year-olds-includes-penis-
pleasure

23 Cassy Fiano-Chesser, "Explosive video: ACLU coaches teachers on how to help
students get secret abortions," Live Action, July 11, 2019, accessed July 30, 2022,
https://www.liveaction.org/news/video-aclu-coaches-teachers-secret-student-a
bortions/.

24 Jeff Johnston, "Austin School District Approves Sexualizing Children Over Parents'
Protests," The Daily Citizen, November 8, 2019, accessed August 2, 2022, https://d
ailycitizen.focusonthefamily.com/austin-school-district-approves-sexualizing-ch
ildren-over-parents-protests/.

25 "Chapter 6: Grades Nine Through Twelve," California Department of Education,
https://www.cde.ca.gov/ci/he/cf/documents/hefwch6gr9-12.docx.

26 Cathy Ruse, "Polyamory is for Pre-Teens in Public Schools. Oh, Really?" The Stream,
July 15, 2019, accessed August 2, 2022, https://stream.org/polyamo-ry-pre-teens-
public-schools-not/.

27 Michelle Cretella, "I'm a Pediatrician. How Transgender Ideology Has Infiltrated
My Field and Produced Large-Scale Child Abuse.," The Daily Signal, July 3, 2017,
accessed August 3, 2022, https://www.daily-signal.com/2017/07/03/im-pediatric
ian-transgender-ideology-infiltrated-field-produced-large-scale-child-abuse/.

28 Austin Ruse and Cathy Ruse, "Fairfax County Votes to Tell Boys They Might be
Girls," The Stream, June 15, 2018, accessed August 3, 2022, https://stream.org/
fairfax-county-votes-tell-boys-might-girls/.

29 Jay Greene Ph.D. "Puberty Blockers, Cross-Sex Hormones, and Youth Suicide."
June 13, 2022, accessed August 3, 2022, https://www.heritage.org/gender/report/
puberty-blockers-cross-sex-hormones-and-youth-suicide

"Hormonal transition" involves giving children as young as 10 years old monthly
injections of Lupron, a "puberty-blocking" intervention. "Cross-sex hormones"
force bodies to develop secondary sex characteristics, like beards on females. Puberty
blockers for "sex transition" have never been tested and are not approved by the
Food and Drug Administration. When they are combined with cross-sex hormones,
they can stunt growth, cause bone fractures, impair memory, and will cause life-long
sterility. The next step in the transition is "sex change" surgery, now called "surgical

affirmation" —the surgical removal of healthy organs and grafting of tissue and muscle to impersonate opposite-sex organs.

30   "Family Life Education Curriculum Advisory Committee Recommendations to the School Board – 2017-2018," Fairfax County Public Schools, https://www.boarddocs .com/vsba/fairfax/Board.nsf/files/AYKU7H699ED9/$file/FLECAC%20Annual% 20Recommendations%20Report%202017_18_051018g.pdf

31   "Planned Parenthood Sex-Ed Not Radical Enough, AISD Proposes Canadian Curriculum to Indoctrinate Children," Texas Values, September 24, 2019, accessed August 4, 2022,

32   "How Are Teachers Trained?," N.C. Values Coalition, accessed August 4, 2022, https://www.ncvalues.org/how_are_teachers_trained.

33   https://downloads.frc.org/EF/EF14C22.pdf

35 "Welcome to Queer America," Teaching Tolerance, https://www.tolerance.org/ podcasts/queer-america/welcome-to-queer-america.

34   Stacy Teicher Khadaroo, "California becomes first state o mandate gay history in curriculum," The Christian Science Monitor, July 14, 2011, accessed August 4, 2022, https://www.csmonitor.com/USA/Educa-tion/2011/0714/California-becomes-first-state-to-mandate-gay-history-in-curriculum.

35   Dan Alexander, "These 12 schools will be first in NJ to teach LGBTQ curriculum," New Jersey 101.5, January 7, 2020, accessed August 2, 2022, https://nj1015.com/ these-12-schools-will-be-first-in-nj-to-teach-lgbtq-curriculum/

36   Joy Pullmann, "How Illinois Schools Teach Preschoolers To Celebrate Transgenderism." October 09, 2019, accessed August 2, 2022, https://thefederalist.com/201 9/10/09/how-illinois-schools-teach-preschoolers-to-celebrate-transgenderism/

About the Author

I worked in show business for over 15 years as an actor, director, producer, casting director, and talent agent. I left that field to go back to school. I received a double B.A. in English and Philosophy (with High Honors) at the University of California, Riverside. I started a double M.A. in Philosophy and Theatre at the University of New Mexico, Albuquerque, with the intention of teaching at the community college level. However, I was recruited to manage the west coast division of Books Are Fun. After ten years, I left BAF to get into teaching. I returned to school and received an MA in Film & Literature from National University in La Jolla, California. I taught English, Economics, History, and Drama from 2007-2018 at Tombstone High School, and Economics, Government, and History at Valley Union HS in Elfrida, AZ. I also taught Philosophy, Film, and English at Cochise College. I'm currently teaching at Pearson Learning and Elevate K-12 Learning